DILEMMA
THE QUOTE BOOK

M. SOSA

First Printing, 2016

ISBN 978-0-9951533-1-8

"It *wasn't* love.
I was just in love with the idea of
who you could potentially be."

*D*edication

My beautiful daughter, I dedicate this book to you because it displays some of my favorite quotes and I know you will find them helpful throughout different stages of your life.

You are the reason I write. You are the reason I breathe. You are my pride and joy. You are my life. Everything I do is for you. I love you.

To You, My Readers

This is my second book, and I cannot describe how excited I am to share it with you. I thank each and every one of you that support my writing on the regular, without you, this would not be possible. To those of you who follow my quotes page on Instagram or Facebook, thank you for taking this journey with me. I am thankful for the opportunity to share my thoughts and past experiences with all of you. You will never understand how much you all mean to me. Thank you from the bottom of my heart. xo

*I*ntroduction

In this book, you will find some of my favorites quotes that will make you smile, make you cry, make you think twice and will make you reminisce on certain moments that impacted your life. I hope they inspire you, motivate you and guide you towards finding whatever you are searching for in life.

Note: Even though, some quotes refer to "he", they do not categorize a specific gender. I am simply writing this book from my perspective so you can switch it to a "she" when needed.

I hope you enjoy these quotes as much as I enjoyed sharing them with you.

"I lost my mind following what my heart wanted, instead of following what it really needed."

"Be with someone who respects you, listens to you, and makes you look forward to tomorrow."

"I found true happiness when I stopped wishing for you to change."

"The day will eventually come when I look you straight in the face and feel nothing."

"I gave you all I had to give and if that wasn't enough, maybe you're the one that's not good enough for me."

"Whenever a relationship fails, it's a sign from the universe telling you that you deserve better than the previous one you were in."

"If you're not worried about me,
why am I wasting my time
worrying about you?"

"My heart eventually got tired of waiting for you to make up your mind about us."

"Sometimes the biggest heartbreak comes from loving someone who will never love you back, and will never give you a chance to prove it."

"My only regret was not finding the courage to leave you earlier."

"Her biggest mistake wasn't loving too hard, but staying too long with someone who never saw her worth."

"Just because you want someone doesn't mean they'll want you too."

"The truth is, I gave you too much of me while you were busy just thinking about you."

"You were never the right fit for me, and I can see that now."

"All I can do is reminisce on the love we once shared, even though I know you probably don't do the same."

"What I loved... it ain't here anymore."

"Stop breaking your own heart for someone who isn't even fighting to keep yours in one piece."

"He isn't worth it if you're not happy."

"I was so busy trying to fix your heart,
that I broke mine in the process."

"I will never compete with anybody for second place."

"You're a part of my past that
I'm never going back to."

"People fall in love so easily but fail to stay there long enough."

"Just because you want him, doesn't mean he deserves you."

"The best lessons come from the people that leave us."

"You can either keep feeling sorry for yourself or you can take control of your life. You choose."

"I never thought the day would come where the thought of you wouldn't cross my mind. I've spent weeks, even months, not thinking about you. Spending my time doing things I missed doing, instead of sobbing over you. No longer wasting my time pondering what could have been, or over thinking why things went wrong. Yes, I learned to live without you... the same way you learned to live without me."

"The love you couldn't give me, I found with someone else. I found a reason to smile again."

"Inconsistency is a major turn off."

"It's ironic how they try to come back into your life when you're ready to move on."

"You're upset because I'm no longer available when you need attention. Yet, every time I needed you, you took me for granted. And now you expect me to be available just because it's convenient for you... What about my needs?"

"When I tell you I love you, I mean every word. I'll fight to make it work even when you feel like you have no energy left. I won't give up easily, no matter what is thrown my way, but if you push me away, I'll walk away knowing I gave it my all."

"I respect myself enough to say "no" to anything that hurts me."

"A real man will never rush you into doing things you're uncomfortable with."

"Growth is letting things
and people go."

"Never become bitter if someone leaves you. Understand that not everybody is meant to stay in your life, and sometimes them leaving is a blessing."

"It's not that I didn't want to give him a second chance. It's the fact that I didn't want to wake up one day regretting my decision, so I chose happincss before anything else. I chose me first."

"As I began to love myself,
my relationship with
everyone changed."

"If lying, cheating and flirting is the way you show love... I don't want it."

"I get tired of being ignored. When you're not giving me the attention I need, I'll eventually not want it anymore."

"My strength comes from all the days I cried for you to come back into my life. The dreadful nights I spent wondering who you were spending them with. The lonely moments I endured laying in my bed consumed with thoughts of disbelief. The heartaches I suffered thinking of you and where we went so wrong. Time changed me into someone who's no longer weak at the thought of you. I no longer feel the need to wait around and see if you'll want me back. I can finally hold my own, and one day, I'll be able to love again."

"I am enough. I am worthy. Now keep repeating that to yourself."

"You left when I needed you most.
No tears, no reason... you just left.
And now, I'm stuck picking up
what is left of me."

"I can't blame you for everything because I knew what I was getting into each time I kept going back. I'm the fool in love."

"Not everybody is your ex. Not everybody will break your heart."

"If he's hiding you from other females, he doesn't care for you as much as you think he does. He's too scared to lose the attention he's getting from them. He feels if he settles down with you and shows that you're "together", all the other females that give him attention will stop. If he isn't able to let go of his childish boy games, move on. You shouldn't be waiting around for a boy who isn't ready to be with a woman like you.

------> Keyword = Boy "

"The more inconsistent you become, the harder you make it to fully love you."

"He leaves a trail of broken women behind him, and you expect him to be different with you when he still hasn't mastered what love really means?"

"I forgive you but I'll never forget."

"I can't wait on you forever. I refuse to stop my life, waiting for you to make a decision because you're unsure if you want a relationship or not. This is not a game. This is my life, my heart and my dignity you are affecting, so make a decision before it's too late."

"If they're not showering you with loyalty and respect, they're not the right ones for you."

"I will never compete with anybody for your attention. If you can't make me a priority, I know where the door is."

"Note to self:

Stop breaking your own heart by letting the wrong person back into your life each time they come knocking. They can't break your heart if they can't get inside."

"Someone will hurt you emotionally, at least once in your lifetime. That person will be reckless with your heart. They will tear it into pieces and will stomp on it without realizing the pain it's causing you. You will feel broken and will feel as though the pain will never end. Even when you are at your lowest, you will learn something new and valuable about yourself. You will learn what self-love is all about and will reach a new level of appreciation for yourself. In due time, you will rise as a new person and will look back at that moment that brought you to tears, and you'll laugh at who you used to be. You will be stronger than ever and will conquer anything and anybody that tries to cause you harm."

"Sometimes, it's not love. Sometimes, it's just infatuation, an addiction. You keep going back to him because you want to feel what he used to make you feel. And there you go falling into the same habit... same trap... all over again. Stop. "

"Saying goodbye is difficult. Never seeing the person you love again is the heartbreaking part."

"Guard your heart. Not everybody should have access to it."

"Love isn't a game. You can't keep coming in and out of my life as you please."

"Never chase anybody. If you know your worth, you should know better than to keep knocking on a door that should have been closed ages ago."

"He doesn't deserve you. The more you do for him, the more he takes advantage of your kindness. And yet, you stay... hoping... wishing...praying that someday he will change. When will you learn to see him for who he really is?"

"You are enough.
You always have been.
You've just given your love to
the wrong person each time."

"When I look in the mirror, I don't recognize the person standing in front of me. I've changed in many ways. I'm resilient and selfless. I no longer fear my past mistakes because I've learned to accept and move past them. My emotional scars are a reminder that I survived some of the deepest wounds. I'm strong now, and I'm prepared to face all challenges that are in the present. My high standards can no longer be overlooked because I refuse to bring them down for anybody. I'm the master of my reality, and no longer a victim of life."

"The more you give a person that doesn't value you, the less they'll respect you. They'll just keeping taking advantage of you, for as long as you allow them to. Time to wake up."

"I loved you. I cherished you. I made you my everything, and all you did was bring me heartbreak after heartbreak. Broken promises every time. You never loved me and I can see that now."

"Letting go doesn't mean you're a quitter. It means you've realized the person you're with is no longer worth your effort and tears."

"Accept the fact that not everything is meant to be. The fear of moving on is holding you back from getting what you deserve, so you settle for simply being comfortable. Don't let that fear win."

"Oh sweetheart! You'll get over him. Don't be so hard on yourself. Time will heal your pain but the longer you keep reminiscing and wondering what could have been, the longer you'll stay stuck in the past."

"You're biggest mistake wasn't loving too hard, but staying too long with someone who never saw your worth."

"You deserve to be number one. You deserve to have someone match your efforts. If they aren't doing that for you—RUN."

"The older you get, the less tolerant you become towards meaningless relationships. You won't allow anybody to waste your time."

"Do I miss him? Yes.
Will I call him? No.
I know better than to keep knocking on
the door from the past. If I keep going
back there, I'm basically telling my
future I'm not ready."

"You owe it to yourself to be happy. Nobody can do it for you because the job relies on you, and only you."

"One of the biggest mistakes a woman can make is to confuse a man that lusts after her, over a man that actually loves her."

"I destroyed myself trying to hold on to what we had."

"The best lessons come from
the people that leave us."

"The more someone lies to you while you keep accepting it, the more they'll keep doing it."

"Show me consistency and I'll show you what loyalty is all about."

"You have no idea of the damage you cause a woman when you leave her without a valid reason. You install a fear in her that whoever comes next will leave her too. Shame on you."

"The day came where I felt the strength to finally leave you. It was an overpowering feeling that pushed me to want better for myself. I needed change, but knew it would only start if I stopped being afraid, and followed my heart towards something greater. I knew I had a journey of self-discovery and self-love; a long road ahead of me but I was determined to do it. I knew once I left, I couldn't look back. You were a part of my life that I would learn from... a lesson indeed."

"Never make a promise you can't keep. A broken promise is exactly identical to a lie. Both can cost you the person you love."

"No. I'm not the same... and I thank you for that. Everything you put me through, trying to bring me down, turned me into the strong person I am today."

"Be with someone who is like a bulletproof vest; ready to protect your heart at all cost."

"You keep ignoring what your mind is telling you because you're more focused on what your heart wants."

"Keep wondering why you're not getting what you deserve when you're still holding on to all the things and people you need to let go of."

"A red flag is a red flag. When your intuition keeps warning you that something doesn't feel right, why do you keep ignoring it?"

"If you're with someone that destroys your happiness and makes you feel as if you're suffocating all the time... LEAVE."

"A strong woman won't hesitate to drop you from the pedestal she has placed you high on, if you start neglecting her. She knows better than to wait around on someone who doesn't value her."

"Stop nagging him. If he's trying his best, let him prove it to you."

"Do you ever feel like you do too much for people all the time, and you neglect to do more for yourself? That's a sign—fix it."

"You cannot fix a broken man if he isn't willing to fix himself first. The more you try to repair the broken pieces of his heart, the more broken-hearted you'll become."

"...but, what if he's actually Mr. Right?"

"If they really loved you, they wouldn't keep hurting you. THAT'S NOT LOVE."

"Losing you made me feel so alone. You were all I could think of when closing my eyes at night, and when waking up in the morning. You were the one I ran to whenever I needed someone to talk to. Your scent on my clothes made it unbearable for me to forget you, but things changed. The day came when I realized you were no longer my everything. You quit when things got rough while I fought to keep our relationship alive. You were weak, I was strong. And I couldn't waste my valuable time thinking of where things went wrong, or how we could try to fix things. It was time to move on... move forward, without you."

"Real relationships aren't perfect. There will be problems. There will be arguments. There will be disagreements. It's how you manage to make things work that makes it perfect in your eyes."

"My mistake was trying to change a man. He wasn't ready, and I tried to force him into something he wasn't capable of giving me."

"Love ends. People move on."

"When you keep giving someone too many chances, the less respect they'll have for you. They won't be afraid to lose you because they know you love them too much to walk away. Set your standards high and stop giving so many chances to someone that keeps playing with your heart."

"Just because I put up with your nonsense in the past does not mean I'm foolish enough to take you back. See, I don't want part-time love. I want someone who will be creative in the ways they love me and whom I won't have to question because I know they're doing right by me even when I'm not around. taking you back would be me taking 10 steps backwards and I refuse to lower my standards ever again."

"...and just like that, every love
song I heard was about you."

"What if I showed you all my flaws when we first met, instead of showing you what you wanted to see? Would you still feel the same way?"

"You'll never be able to change someone that doesn't see a problem with their actions."

"Every time I look into your eyes, I see my future."

"Lie after lie after lie, I stayed. Maybe I'm a fool in love or maybe I just don't know any better because I've never had anybody treat me with the respect I deserve."

"Sometimes "I'm Sorry" isn't enough."

"Once you take the time to love and find yourself, the right one will find you."

"It's not about you. It's not about me. It's about "us". We have to have a common goal if we want to grow together."

"When a woman's fed up, she will stop doing all the things she used to do. She will no longer care for you the way she used to, or cater to you when you expect her to. She won't even show any remorse on the way she's treating you because you've put her through so much crap during the time you've been together. She won't see a point in even acknowledging why she is acting the way she is. She will remain silent and oblivious to any of your needs. She will no longer make you her priority. No, she will start focusing her energy on herself and make sure that she is happy in every aspect of her life. She will no longer worry if you've eaten or if you're missing anything. She will show you what it feels like to miss her."

"You deserve to be happy, no excuses. Never allow yourself to be *kind of* or *partially* loved."

THE MISTAKES OF A WOMAN

VOLUME 1
A LESSON LEARNED

AVAILABLE NOW!

THE MISTAKES OF A WOMAN

VOLUME 2
A NEW BEGINNING

....COMING WINTER 2017!

CONTACT

Email

iammaggiesosa@hotmail.com

Social Media

Instagram:
www.instagram.com/sweetzthoughts

Facebook:
www.facebook.com/sweetzthoughts

Dilemma: The Quote Book - 2016

306.7 SOSA
Sosa, M.,
Dilemma :

OCT 0 2 2017

CPSIA information can be obtained
at www.ICGtesting.com
Printed in the USA
LVOW05s0608240717
542396LV00006B/32/P

9 780995 153318